WHO KNEW?
SUPER SAVING TIPS

D0095687

WHO KNEW?
SUPER SAVING TIPS

BY JEANNE BOSSOLINA LUBIN
AND
BRUCE LUBIN

REDUCE YOUR DEBT TODAY

SAVE $200 AT THE SUPERMARKET

TAX SAVING TIPS

FREE STUFF

MUCH, MUCH MORE!

Castle Point
Publishing

Printed in China

Cover and interior design Quadrum Solutions Pvt. Ltd
ISBN: 978-0-9820667-1-3

DEDICATION

To Jack, Terrence, and Aidan, as always

ACKNOWLEDGEMENTS

We're grateful to our families for putting up with us while we wrote this book, particularly to our three boys for their good humor as we missed more than a few soccer matches, basketball games, and other events. Kids, this isn't the first time your parents will disappoint you—get used to it. Once again, James Tavendale pulled a rabbit out of his hat and has proven to be an indispensable resource. Karen Matsu Greenberg has forgotten more about printing books than we'll ever know, and we're thankful for her for keeping us on track with our schedules. Joy Mangano has been a good friend and inspiration, and we'll always be grateful for her boundless energy, words of encouragement and sound advice. Joanie Rudolph and Andrea Cajuste have guided us through the scary, scary world of shipping, logistics and stickering, and imparted so much information to us that we thought our heads would explode (which we would have cleaned up with club soda and vinegar, naturally). Thanks, ladies, for not laughing at us as we asked a series of dim-bulb questions. The team at Quadrum Solutions have done a remarkable job designing and typesetting this book, and we're still scratching our heads and wondering how they manage to work 27 hours a day. Finally, special thanks to Brian Scevola, who suggested we write this book in the first place, and offered enthusiastic guidance throughout the entire process. Brian, you handled every setback and delay with good humor and patience (and maybe just a little profanity), and for that we're grateful.

CONTENTS

CHAPTER 1
HOW TO REDUCE YOUR
DEBT BY HALF
9

CHAPTER 2
FREE MOVIES, MUSIC,
TV, AND MORE
15

CHAPTER 3
CHEAP VACATIONS AND
FAMILY ACTIVITIES
21

CHAPTER 4
HOW TO SAVE $200 OFF
YOUR GROCERY BILL
29

CHAPTER 5
GET DRESSED FOR LESS
35

CHAPTER 6
BEAUTY ON A BUDGET   41

CHAPTER 7
TAX-SAVING TIPS   47

CHAPTER 8
SAVINGS FOR YOUR
HOUSE AND CAR   53

CHAPTER 9
MORE FREE STUFF   61

CHAPTER 10
OTHER WAYS TO MAKE
MONEY AND SAVE   71

HOW TO REDUCE YOUR DEBT BY HALF

UP YOUR CREDIT SCORE

It's a tough time to get credit, so make sure your rating is as good as possible. Here are a few easy ways to raise your credit score.

• If you haven't already, get a free credit report by going to Annualcreditreport.com or calling 1-877-322-8228. Don't be fooled by other "Free Credit Report" sites, which often require you to pay a membership fee.

• Check your report for accuracy. On the internet, you can often click the item directly to dispute it. Make sure all of the addresses listed are current or former addresses, and that all loans and lines of credit listed are yours. If you're unsure, contact the customer service number on the report and ask for more information.

• Get rid of credit cards you never use anymore. See three or four credit cards for stores you don't frequently shop at? Even if you don't carry balances on these cards, one of the things that can lower your credit rating is the amount of available credit you have. Call the number on the back of the cards and cancel them!

• If you are listed as a secondary card holder for an account of someone who's racked up a lot of money on the card, this can negatively impact your credit rating. If it isn't necessary for you to be on this credit card account, call the company and get your name taken off.

DUE DATES

Here's an easy solution if you keep getting socked with late fees, or neglect to pay more than the minimum on your credit cards because the payment is always due at the same time as your rent. Ask your credit card company to change the date your payment is due. It might take a few months to kick in, but you'll be able to pay down the card more easily during the part of the month that isn't as much of a crunch.

• You can request a free credit report once a year. Try to make a regular habit of requesting it and reviewing it as closely as you would your bank statement. The more quickly you notice a discrepancy, the easier it will be to get it removed from your report.

MAKE SURE YOU KNOW THE FACTS

Always read the terms of a credit card agreement before you sign up for the card. The fine print may be boring, but you owe it to yourself to make sure you're not getting a bum deal. Highlight any passages you don't understand, and find out what they mean by asking a lawyer or accountant; or simply look the phrase up in an internet search engine. Some agreements will try to scam you—one recent ploy is for companies to buy up your bad debt, then trick you into signing up for a card that already has the bad debt tacked onto the balance. (If this happens to you, you should insist on getting documents that prove that you are accountable for that debt or the interest, so don't agree to anything until you speak with that lawyer or accountant.) Be especially careful if the offer seems too good to be true.

GOOD GUIDANCE

If you feel like you're in over your head with your debt, or if you simply want some answers about the most efficient way to pay it off and manage a budget, there is free counseling available to you. These one-on-one sessions are offered by organizations across the country who want to help people who are struggling with money problems. They also often offer consolidation loans and debt management programs. To find an agency that will work with you in person, over the phone, online, or via mail, call the National Foundation for Credit Counseling—an organization that makes sure its members are accredited, not-for-profit, and generally on the level—at 1-800-388-2227.

WHO KNEW?
According to the Federal Reserve Board, Americans have $2.56 trillion in consumer debt.

BRING IT TOGETHER

Debt consolidation is a smart and relatively painless way to ease some of the hardship of having lots of debt. With debt consolidation, you can lower your monthly payments, and you may also be able to lock in a lower interest rate. The easiest kinds of consolidations to obtain are for student loans, but many banks also offer consolidation services for mortgages, and (if your credit score is good) credit card debt. There are different types of debt consolidation services, so make sure you know what you're getting into. Some services—often non-profits—contact the financial institutions you owe the money to and try to get your interest rates lowered. Then you pay them one lump payment each month, and they pay the companies for you. Other types of debt consolidation—usually through banks—basically just give you a loan to pay off all your other loans. Either way, debt consolidation can make your finances a little more manageable.

BECAUSE COLLEGE SHOULDN'T BREAK THE BANK

If your child (or grandchild) is finally heading to college, make sure you take advantage of all the free money and discounted loans that are out there to support you. Check out Princetonreview.com or Petersons.com to find searchable lists of grants from the lofty (a National Merit scholarship) to the small and silly ($500 for speaking Klingon). For local awards and scholarship contests, make sure to check the newspaper and at the high school counselor's office for opportunities. Finally, if you know what college your son or daughter is attending, make sure you have an up-to-date lists of all merit- and need-based grants and loans it offers. If you think you may qualify, don't be afraid to call up the school's registrar or financial aid department and ask for more information.

CHOOSING THE CARD THAT'S RIGHT FOR YOU

Even if you're in the market for a new credit card, the amount of offers that show up in your mailbox can be daunting. And whether you anticipate your relationship with the card to be long and prosperous, or quick and a little irresponsible, how do you know which card is right for you? Here are some questions to ask before you decide.

• How long is the introductory period? Most cards start you off with a good deal, like low APR or free balance transfers. But make sure to check how long the promotional rates lasts.

• What perks does it have? If you fly a lot, cards with air-mile programs can save you hundreds. Other cards offer insurance on purchases or car rentals. Figure out how much you think these extras will save you, and take this into consideration when you pick a card.

• What will your credit limit be? Most companies don't like to tell you what your credit limit is until you apply for the card, but before you sign, first ask them how much you are going to be able to spend. If you're good about paying your bill off, having a high percentage of credit left will help your credit score. But if you have trouble not maxing out, ask if you can lower the card's limit.

• What's the best deal you can get? Compare card offers and don't be afraid to negotiate. Visit Cardweb.com, where you can find hundreds of cards sorted by types of rewards, your credit history, and their brand. Call the phone number listed to see if you qualify for cards that fit what you need.

WHAT TO DO WHEN COLLECTION AGENCIES CALL

Nothing feels worse than having collection agencies calling you all of the time. If you have old debt, it's time to stop feeling bad about it and confront the collection agencies or credit card companies head-on. Here are some tips for dealing with debt in collections, one of the worst kinds in terms of your credit report.

• The first step is to stop ignoring phone calls and letters. It's hard, but you know it must be done!

• It's important to remember the person you're talking to is just doing his or her job. If you're polite during the entire call, he or she will be more likely to help you out. Whatever you do, don't lose your cool.

• The first tactic of most collection agencies will be to try to get you to pay the total amount at once. You should be aware that you can always set up a payment plan. Only pay as much as you think you can each month—never commit to more than you can pay and risk being unable to make payments.

• Most collection agencies will settle for 40 to 60 percent of the total amount you owe. The more you can pay them immediately as a lump sum, and the higher you can make your monthly payments, the better! Don't be afraid to negotiate.

• In local and state courts in many areas, lawsuits from collection and credit card agencies have

IT'S TIME FOR A TRANSFER

If you owe lots of money to one credit card and not-so-much to one with a lower interest rate, ask your credit card company if you can do a balance transfer. You may incur a fee, but you often end up saving in the end, and many cards offer them for free during the first year of your agreement. If you have two cards from the same company, ask if the card with the better deal allows "credit reallocation," which would let you transfer not only the balance from the other card but its credit limit as well, without even submitting you to another credit check.

ASK AND YOU SHALL RECEIVE

It sounds too simple to be true, but one of the first things you should do when attempting to reduce your debt is call up your credit card company and ask them to reduce your interest rate or annual percentage rate (APR). If you have had the card for a while and have routinely made payments on time, the company is usually happy to take this piece-of-cake step to keep your business.

been overturned. If you are being asked to pay more than 60 percent of the debt, the agency has been unable to show you proof that you owe the debt, or you otherwise feel like you're getting a raw deal, don't be afraid to go to court with the collection agency. Not only do you deserve to go in front of a neutral arbitrator, it will it make the other party more likely to settle (because they won't want to pay lawyer's fees). However, it is vitally important that you stay apprised of court dates and show up to every one of them.

• Stay empowered! Remember the important thing: you're taking care of your bad debt. You deserve to be able to work towards clean credit, and to have the agency you owe money to be polite and respectful. Don't settle for less!

SAVE, THEN SPEND

As Veruca Salt said in *Willy Wonka and the Chocolate Factory,* "I want it, and I want it now!" It's hard to break ourselves of buying expensive items when we want them, then paying them off over the next several months. But saving up ahead of time has numerous benefits.

• First of all, you'll make sure you really want the item. Having to save up for six months for a new TV will give you plenty of time to reconsider if the old 20" is good enough. And trust us, once you do finally have the money it feels so much better to go home with a piece of merchandise that's bought and paid for, rather than one that has just put you farther in the hole.

• When you start up a new store credit card to pay for a big-ticket item, this credit card will pop up on your credit report as being opened and immediately maxed out. Obviously, this isn't good news for your credit score.

• Finally, not having to pay something off after the fact means no interest payments. And many mom-and-pop stores will give you a lower price if you pay all in cash.

chapter 2

FREE MOVIES, MUSIC, TV, AND MORE

WHERE THE WILD FILES ARE

MP3s are music files you can play on your computer. Pretty much any computer these days comes with some kind of program to play MP3s, and MP3s files are easy to find on the internet. You should be aware, though, that many sites that offer free MP3s aren't legal, as there are laws in place to make sure that studios and artists get money for their songs. Here are some sites, however, where you can find free, legal MP3 files to download.

• Amazon.com offers dozens of free MP3s as special promotions. To find them, simply select "MP3 downloads" from the drop-down search menu. When the list pops up, select "Price: low to high" from the drop-down sort menu on the upper right-hand side of the MP3 list. You can also subscribe to an email newsletter than keeps you apprised of new deals—keep an eye out for the "Amazon delivers" ad on the left side of the screen and click on "subscribe now."

• If stress is getting you down, head over to Musicrelaxation.com and click on "Free relaxation mp3." Then download, play, and kick back with a glass of wine.

• If you're a fan of old radio shows like *Amos & Andy, Bing* Crosby specials, and the *Benny Goodman Show,* check out Radiolovers.com, which gives you free downloads of hundreds of classic programs.

• If you use iTunes, check the iTunes store regularly for free tracks, which you can easily find on the main page or the music home page.

• For easy-to-download MP3s of all varieties, go to Sideloader.com, which pulls MP3s from free sources from around the internet.

WHO KNEW?

Concessions such as pop corn, candy, and soda account for 40 percent of a movie theater's revenue.

ONLINE MOVIES AND TV FOR FREE

At Truveo.com, you can find literally hundreds of movies you can watch for free. While many of them are kind of weird (like "The Giant Gilla Monster"), there are some hits you've never seen and plenty of classics you'll love to watch again, like "The Man Who Knew Too Much" and "Nobody's Fool." Do a search for "full length movie" to sift out the clips. For TV shows, try Hulu.com or the website of the network the show airs on.

JUST DON'T OPEN HER BOX

Pandora.com is nothing short of amazing. It's an online radio station that tailors what it plays to what you like, and it's almost scarily accurate. Better yet, it will introduce you to tons of artists you never knew existed, but love. It works by streaming the music from your web browser (you don't download any music files), and allowing you to rate songs "thumbs up" or "thumbs down." For every song you rate thumbs up, it will play more like it, and also provide you with a link to where you can purchase the MP3 file online. The downside to Pandora is that you can only skip to the next song six times an hour, and you can't necessarily choose what song or artist you'd like to hear. However, you'll be so pleased with Pandora's music experience customized just for you, you won't mind.

TONS OF FREE BOOKS

No one likes to throw away a book. Therefore, it's easy to find places that give away books or offer them for a dollar or less. Check with your community's recycling center to see if they offer free books that people have thrown in their bin, and ask your local library if they ever

FILMS FOR FREE

Many museums and colleges over free screenings of films. Sure, they're not the latest big releases, but if you're in the mood for a classic or artsy flick, check and see if they are offered nearby. Many facilities even have full-sized screens in auditoriums. And they won't get angry if you sneak in your own candy!

MORE THAN JUST BOOKS

Obviously, libraries are full of books you can borrow for free. But did you know that many libraries also carry DVDs? If there is a particular movie or TV show you are looking for and it's not available at your local branch, ask a librarian to get it for you through inter-library loan. Libraries are also a great place to get magazines. If you don't mind reading back issues, save your subscriptions by getting older copies at the library. This is especially great for kids' magazines (because kids won't know the difference!).

CABLE: NOT ALWAYS A RIP-OFF

If you have cable, you may have movies and television shows available on-demand for free. Many cable systems offer a wide variety of old movies, as well as recent TV shows that cable channels are trying to promote. Every system is different, but take a look and see if there is an option on your On-Demand menu that says "Free Movies," "Free Shows," or "Free On-Demand." You may also have to look through the shows and see which are listed as $0.

have book sales. It's worth it to check out used bookstores, too, which usually have romance novels and paperbacks at cheap prices. Online, go to Paperbackswap.com or Freecycle.org, which will allow you to exchange your books with ones you've never read before.

RENT ON THE CHEAP

What would the weekend be without a trip to the video store? With so many options for movie and video game rental, the supply is up, so it's time to demand! Compare rates at your local video stores, and see if the store with the best perks—like being close to your home and letting you rent for the longest amount of time—will match the lowest price you can find. Since fewer and fewer people have VCRs these days, if you are still renting VHS cassettes, see if you can get a discount or a longer rental period when renting tapes rather than DVDs. Finally, keep an eye out for "redbox" machines, which can be found in many drug and discount stores, where you can rent a DVD for one night for as low as $1.

I'VE BEEN MEANING TO CATCH THAT ONE!

The easiest place to get free DVDs may be at the homes of your friends! Try starting a movie-lending circle with friends or neighbors who also watch movies. Each person has another person they give movies to, and someone they receive them from. When you get your own movie back, it's time to pick a new one! You may want to pick a timeframe to exchange the movie—for example, sometime before each weekend or at a weekly book club or school-related meeting. Movie-lending circles are a great way to discover movies you might not have picked out yourself, but really enjoy.

NOT JUST FOR THE WEB-SAVVY

You've probably heard of Netflix.com, where you pay a low monthly fee and receive unlimited DVDs in the mail, then watch and return them in postage-paid envelopes. But did you realize you don't need a computer to use the service? The company's well-staffed call center will set you up for an account, add movies to your queue, and even make recommendations for movies you might like. Best of all, you get patched through directly to a person—no sifting through automated menus and then waiting for a half-hour. You can reach Netflix 24 hours a day at 1-866-716-0414.

WHAT'S THIS PODCAST THING THE KIDS HAVE BEEN TALKING ABOUT?

Simply put, podcasts are radio shows that can be downloaded for free on the web. If you have iTunes or similar software, check it to see if it offers a podcast search. Otherwise, head over to Podcastalley.com, which will allow you to search for and browse from thousands of podcasts in such genres as comedy, food & drink, and kids & family. It also has links for free podcast-playing software if you don't already have some on your computer. And as your kids may have shown you, podcasts can also be videos, usually up to 15 minutes in length. On the next page are some of our favorite podcasts. To find them, simply enter their names in the search box!

FILL UP BEFORE YOU GO

Even if you don't plan on getting snacks at the theater, if you show up with an empty stomach it's hard to say "no" once you smell that popcorn popping! Always eat before you arrive, that way you'll be safe from snacking—and from spending.

• NPR Story of the Day. This podcast is the best short piece from National Public Radio each day. These are as varied as NPR's programming—one day it will be about extreme pumpkin carving, and the next it will be about missionaries in Kenya. Either way, you know you're going to get something interesting.

• Car Talk. Another podcast from National Public Radio, this show offers two jovial guys from Boston taking call-in questions about car repair. Addicting even if you don't have wheels!

• Stuff You Should Know. Kids as well as adults will get a kick out of this podcast from the website How Stuff Works. Each show tackles a burning question, such as "Will Robots Marry?" and "How Could Cats Scuba Dive?"

• The Onion News Network. This satirical news show, from the makers of newspaper spoof *The Onion,* will have you laughing out loud.

• National Geographic's Wild Chronicles. This video podcast shows digital shorts about wildlife from all over the world. The only downside is that your child will probably act like a spider monkey, a Panama Golden Frog, or whatever else they saw for the rest of the day.

• PBS's Wired Science. From one of the coolest magazines ever, *Wired,* comes this video podcast for geeks. You won't be able to resist finding out how an astronaut's suit works, how to make bottle rockets out of 2-liter bottles, or other nerdy info.

• If you need to divert the kids for a few minutes, try one of Nick Jr.'s podcasts like Blues Clues or Diego. They're each only about a minute long, but luckily kids can watch them a few times in a row…

3

CHEAP VACATIONS AND FAMILY ACTIVITIES

BE A DAY-TRIPPER

The most expensive part of any vacation is transportation and lodging, so consider taking several day trips during the summer rather than one week-long one. Commuter rail lines often offer discounts on train fare and tickets to nearby attractions, or you may be overdue to take a drive to that nearby state park. For ideas of where to take day trips in your area, call your state's tourist board or type your state's name and "day trips" into a search engine.

VISITING HOURS

Even if they normally have high admission prices, most museums offer opportunities for you to visit for free. If a museum gets money from the government, they're usually required to either offer free admission one day a week or charge admission as a "suggestion donation"—i.e., you only have to pay what you want. Other museums have late hours that are free to visitors once a week or month. If you like looking at art, also check out galleries, where you can find cool, local art displayed for free in the hopes that someone will buy it.

THE CHEAPEST RENTAL CARS

When looking for great deals, Hotwire.com is a good place to turn. The downside to this site is that you don't know which airline you're flying or which hotel you're staying at until after you've booked. While we aren't always a fan of this format for flights or lodging, for cars, who cares what dealer it is, as long as it's at the airport?

TV: LIVE AND IN-PERSON!

If you live near a big city, especially Los Angeles or New York, one of the most fun free activities you can do is attend a TV taping. Talk shows, sitcoms, and game shows are always looking for studio audience members, and it's fun to not only see a show live, but get a peek at what happens behind the scenes. To get tickets to shows, visit Tvtickets.com for shows in LA, or Nycvisit.com/content/index.cfm?pagePkey=376 for shows in

New York. Nytix.com offers an even wider range of New York tapings, but requires you pay $3.00 to take advantage of their "special relationships" with the shows. If there is a show you know is taped in your area, try looking it or its network up online or seeing if there is a phone number at the end of the show to call for audience tickets.

THE FIVE-DAY OUTLOOK

Farecast.com is one of our favorite sites when planning a trip. If your travel dates are flexible, it will tell you the cheapest days to travel. If you know exactly when you're coming or going, it will predict whether or not the price will go up or down. The coolest part is, it's not affiliated with a particular airline or site, so the advice is unbiased. If you want to lock in the price the site gives you, you can buy "insurance" for a small fee.

ALSO GREAT FOR LAST-MINUTE DEALS

If you're looking for the best deals in travel, head over to Airfarewatchdog.com, which catalogs the cheapest fares as they are listed on travel sites and airline's sites—including JetBlue and Northwest, which are often not found elsewhere. This site requires a bit of work—you have to click-through to other sites and try to find the rate yourself, but the "watch dog" will tell you which days of the week to search and in what date range. If you normally spend a lot of time trying different combinations of travel dates and nearby airports, this site will take a lot of the guesswork out of it for you.

THE LOVE BOAT

If you're dying to get away on a cruise, check out Cruisedeals.com, which has packages to Alaska, the Bahamas, Hawaii, Mexico, and just about anywhere else you'd want to go on a boat. The company negotiates with some of the world's biggest lines to bring their customers the best rates on cruises. If you want to hit the water, this is the best place to start.

GREAT THINGS COME WITH EDUCATION

If you're 26 or under, you have all the luck. Not only do your knees never get sore and people still try to flirt with you, but you can also get great deals when you're traveling in Europe. If you're aged 12–26, if you're a student of any age, or you're a teacher or faculty member, you qualify for the International Student ID Card. Available at ISEcard.com, the card costs $25, but with it you get discounts on trains, rental cards, tourist attractions, and more. Best of all, they'll provide medical travel insurance up to $2,000.

TIME TO GET A PASSPORT

In these bad economic times, it's hard to see a silver lining, but here's one for anyone who loves an exotic vacation: it's now cheaper than ever to travel to many fascinating destinations around the world like Reykjavik, Iceland; Montreal, Canada; and Sydney, Australia. Check out vacation packages on sites like Expedia.com and Orbitz.com or ask a travel agent for hot deals to faraway lands.

LET'S MAKE A DEAL

When digging for discounts on rental cars and hotels, always call the hotel or rental company directly for the best deals. If the only phone number you have is a national, toll-free one, look up the local number for that particular location and speak to them directly instead. The closer you get to your travel date, the better—in fact, don't be afraid to call the day before to confirm your reservation and ask for a better rate.

BECAUSE A GOOD GAME IS A GOOD GAME

If you love going to see sports, but don't love the price tag of taking your whole family to a professional game, consider amateur sports instead. Colleges as well as intramural leagues have games every weekend for free or a couple of dollars. It's great to support local teams, and younger kids won't even know the difference in skill between a pro player and a Division Three league anyway.

AND YOU GET TO HAVE S'MORES

Waking up to the sights, sounds, and smells of the forest can be one of the most peaceful things you've ever experienced—not to mention, the most inexpensive vacation you've taken in years. If you've never gone camping, it's time to start! If you don't have any equipment, ask friends who do if you can borrow theirs in exchange for lending them something of yours. You and your kids will enjoy working together while roughing it (and don't worry, "roughing it" can involve bathrooms and showers, electricity hook-ups, and even wireless internet). Best of all, with all that hard work each day, plus all the room to run around in, your kids will get exhausted fast! To find campsites across the

GIVE A LITTLE TO GET A LITTLE

Many concert venues, theaters, and museums hire volunteers in exchange for free admission. Doing a bit of volunteer work will help you get away from the kids for a bit and meet new people. Then bring your family back for the savings!

United States and Canada, visit Reserveamerica. com, and for a great article for first-time campers, go to Roadandtravel.com/adventuretravel/ campingforfirsttimers.htm.

PLAY HOOKY!

Sometimes, vacation is all in your mind. If you can't afford to get away but you feel like you're ready to scream, consider taking a personal day off work, and convince your spouse or a friend to do it, too! Then enjoy an empty mall, a relaxing afternoon at a park, or just a huge brunch (complete with mimosas). Whatever you do, get out of your house (which will just remind you of all your chores), and have fun! You'll be surprised how refreshed you feel after a day away.

THE THEME: SAVINGS

Nothing's more fun than taking the kids to an amusement park, especially when they've been begging you to do it for two summers now. Whether you're going to a local, Six Flags type of park, or going all out for that Disneyland vacation, here are some tips to keep your costs down.

• A lot of organizations offer discount packages to local and national theme parks. Check with any organizations you belong to, such as the AARP, AAA, wholesale clubs like BJ's or Costco, or a branch of the military. Also look for promotions mailed out with your credit card bill.

• Ask for a group discount. If you have at least 15 people in your party, you can usually get a good deal, depending on the time of year.

WHO KNEW?

According to the Travel Industry Association, the number of trips taken drops by around 15 percent from summer to fall.

• Visit AmusementPark.com, which has great deals on tickets to amusement parks around the country. They also have savings on local tours, dinner cruises, museums, and tourist attractions.

• Keep an eye out for merchandise tie-ins. Many products—especially soda and chips—offer easy discounts such as bringing the wrapper or can to the park to get several dollars off.

• Check out the packages. Large theme parks such as Universal Studios and Disney World always offer package deals on—for example—a flight, hotel, and park tickets. These aren't usually significantly cheaper than buying tickets online through a site like Expedia.com or Orbitz.com, but they do often offer added incentives like free transportation or breakfasts.

• Call the park and ask them! Most parks (or their automated representative) will tell you about current deals being offered, and may offer promotions of their own. Also check the website for the individual park you're visiting.

• Before you get to the park, consider the real money-wasters: food and souvenirs. Bring lunches from home, and give each child a certain amount they are allowed to spend at gift shops. For more indecisive kids afraid of hitting their limit, make sure to offer them the chance to go back for an item in a store if they don't find anything they like more (they usually will).

FORGO THE FOILAGE

The best summer vacation you'll ever take might not be in the summer. As soon as Labor Day goes by, the rates go down drastically on hotels and airfare to most vacation destinations. Some of the most-discounted areas are the Caribbean, Hawaii, California, and anywhere there's a beach. In a warm climate, it will still be as hot as ever on the sand. But the price will be much less and you get the added benefit of having fewer crowds. Check out a travel site like Travelocity.com for good deals to your dream destinations.

NOTES

4

HOW TO SAVE $200 OFF YOUR GROCERY BILL

SAVINGS IN NUMBERS

This one's a no-brainer: always buy in bulk. If you're not a member of a discount wholesaler like Sam's Club or Costco, offer to drive a friend who is a member to use his or her discount. They'll save on gas, and you'll save on all sorts of food and supplies for the house. And don't forget that giant, 10-pound package of toilet paper.

BREAK FREE FROM BRANDS

When you've been buying the same brand of product since you can remember, it's hard to make the switch to generics. However, you'll be surprised when you find many generic and store-brand products taste exactly the same (or better!) for less than half the cost.

• Always buy generic baking ingredients such as flour, oil, and sugar. These generics are indistinguishable from their more-expensive counterparts. Frozen and canned vegetables are also usually exactly the same.

• As for products such as cereals, cookies, and crackers, basic is better—we've had good luck with plain granola, potato chips, and wheat crackers.

• No matter what the product, it never hurts to try. If you end up having to throw away one can of soup, you've wasted a couple of dollars, but if you like it, you can save a lot over a year.

• Save the boxes from name-brand products your kids are attached to, then empty the generic products into them. Your picky eaters won't know the difference if they can't see it on the outside.

DON'T FORGET YOUR COUPONS

Save the tedium from sifting through the Sunday paper and circulars by finding your coupons on the web. There are literally dozens of websites that allow you to print out coupons and take them right to the store. Our favorite is Couponmom.com, which has an amazing array of grocery deals by state, manufacturers' coupons, and even links for free samples online. Coupons.smartsource.com is also a great site that shows you the new coupons first, so if you visit frequently you won't have to wade through ones you've already seen. Couponclippers.com *sells* coupons—which may sound crazy, but they're sold for a small fraction of their face value. This site has a fantastic selection (as it should—you're paying for it!) and even sells expired coupons if you shop at one of those free-wheeling grocery stores.

GO FOR THE BIG HAUL
Buying lots of groceries in one trip rather than a few groceries in several trips is better for your wallet. Not only do you save on gas money, but according to a study by the Marketing Science Institute, shoppers who are only making a quick trip to the store purchase an average of 54 percent more than they had planned. In addition to visiting the store less frequently, make a grocery list before you go to make sure you cut down on impulse buys.

THE BEST THINGS COME TO THOSE WHO WAIT
Here's a great tip if you find yourself balking at spending the time to clip coupons just to save 50¢ here or there. Cut out coupons from the Sunday paper, then let them sit for four weeks. Many food and cosmetic companies plan their promotions so that customers buy their products right when the coupons are released. Often, these products are put on sale 3-4 weeks after the coupon appears in the paper. If you wait to use your coupons, you'll find that they often sync up with an in-store promotion, so you'll save twice as much.

RE-USE BEFORE YOU RECYCLE
There are a lot of "disposable" products that can actually be washed and re-used to save you money. Instead of throwing them away after one use, use Ziploc bags, vacuum bags, take-out containers, plastic silverware, and water and juice

NOT GOOD ENOUGH FOR THE MARKET... BUT GOOD ENOUGH FOR US

Many food manufacturers such as Pepperidge Farm, Hostess, and Sara Lee have special "thrift shops" that sell products that are after their sell-by dates, but still perfectly good. These stores are a way for the manufacturers to make a bit of money, and for you to save big—usually 50 percent or more. If you know there is a plant or headquarters for a grocery brand in your area, call and inquire about thrift shops or look up locations in the yellow pages or online.

bottles again and again. Just make sure to wash them thoroughly each time, and you shouldn't re-use Ziploc bags if you've had meat or other foods susceptible to bacteria in them. You'll feel good about saving and doing something "green" around the house!

NEVER PAY A DOLLAR FOR A LEMON AGAIN

It may be a pain, but the best way to save on groceries is to shop at more than one market. You'll soon find that one store will have cheaper produce, one will have cheaper meat, and so forth. Explore grocery stores you've never shopped at—perhaps one that is closer to your workplace or gym rather than by your home—and you may find even lower prices. We've even found cheaper products at stores that are the same chain, just a different location. Write down the prices of your most frequently purchased items, or bring a receipt from an average grocery trip with you. That way you can be sure to remember where the prices are the most reasonable.

A TRICK WORTHY OF THE LUCKY CHARMS LEPRECHAUN

If you're one of those super-parents who don't let their kids eat sugary cereal, have you thought about using it as a reward? Kids not used to having a morning sugar fix normally like sugary cereal brands as much as they like candy, so why not use it instead? That way, when kids are getting a sugary treat for being good, they'll at least getting it from a food that is also enriched with vitamins. And if you've been wanting to wean your children off the sugary stuff in the morning, this might be a good way to start!

WHO KNEW?

Most Americans drink about 57 gallons of soft drinks per year. Soft drinks are the leading source of calories for most people. Substitute soda for water and you'll not only save, you'll lose weight!

KNOW WHAT YOU'RE GETTING

Before you're convinced to buy something because it's on sale, make sure to carefully consider the discount offer. For example, when something is offered for 25 percent off, with an additional 25 percent taken at the register, you're usually not actually getting 50 percent off—you're getting 25 percent of 25 percent—or 43.75 percent off. Also, make sure to ask whether "buy one, get one free" promotions require you to purchase two items, or if you can simply get one for 50 percent off. Finally, be aware that many stores put quantity limits on sale items just to try to convince consumers that the product is in demand. Buying more than you regularly would doesn't save you money—it makes them more.

STOCK UP

When carving a chicken or turkey, it's easy to make a stock at the same time. Place all unused parts in a pot with celery and onion (using the skins of the onion will give the stock a nice, rich color), then heat up to boiling. Reduce the heat and simmer while you make dinner. Stock can be used for gravies, made into soup (naturally), and used to flavor rice, potatoes, and tomato sauce. This free and easy seasoning would have cost you up to $5 for a quart at the grocery store!

SPICE UP YOUR LIVES

Here's a fun way to save money on your grocery bill while also coercing the kids into helping you around the house: grow a spice garden. Getting even a small variety of easy-to-grow herbs such as basil, mint, oregano, and thyme can save money and give you fresher ingredients to work with (and for a treat for your feline friends, try cat nip, too!) . Find the seeds at a home and garden store,

BIGGER IS BETTER

Meat is expensive enough, but part of the cost is the price you're paying the butcher to cut it up for you. Buy the largest cuts of meat you can, then cut up, wrap in foil, and freeze inside a plastic bag in your freezer. When purchasing chicken, joint the bird by slicing along fat lines (or type "cutting a chicken" into google for more detailed instructions), then cook whole. Cooked chicken lasts a long time and is great for adding to salads, soups, and stir-frys.

or buy the small plants at a nursery or farmer's market. Get the kids involved by putting the plants somewhere they can reach, and helping them water them when necessary. Add the leaves—either fresh or dried—to elevate simple dishes to the next level. If your kids really get into it, you may even convince them to do a vegetable garden next year!

CAN IT

Save at the store by going canned—all recipes except for salads can be made with canned vegetables instead of the fresh ones. As long as you check the ingredients to make sure sugar hasn't been added, any vegetable in a can will taste nearly indistinguishable from a fresh one you cooked yourself, especially if they're going into sauces or casseroles.

LOOK DOWN!

When shelving items, grocery stores customarily put the least expensive items on the bottom shelves. That's because most customers, when looking for a particular product, will just take the first item they see—at eye-level. When at the market, make sure to check the lower shelves for lower prices.

NEVER PAY FOR A MILK BONE AGAIN

When getting a "treat" for being good, most dogs are just excited about a special snack, not that it's in the shape of a bone. The truth is, doggie treats have almost the exact same ingredients as dog food, and most dogs can't tell the difference. Instead of paying extra for dog treats, keep a separate container of dog food where you normally keep the treats, then give your dog a small handful when he's done something reward-worthy.

GET DRESSED FOR LESS

chapter

5

KEEP IT SIMPLE

When you're buying clothes, always go for classic looks rather than modern, stylized ones. A blue v-neck t-shirt will be fashionable year after year, while something with more exotic colors or patterns will go out of style quickly. Buying more basic clothing will make sure you don't have to buy as many new articles of clothing each season.

THE SEASONAL SHOPPING SECRET

For the best deals on clothes, always shop in the off-season. Buy spring and summer clothing in July and August, and fall and winter clothing in January and February. (You can often find the best sales right after the holiday season.) It's sometimes a bummer to buy something you're not going to be able to wear for six months, but when the time comes to switch seasons you'll be happy you already have some new clothes to wear—all of which were purchased on sale!

A TRICK FROM A PROFESSIONAL

We'll never forget a friendly repairman who was fixing our washing machine who told us, "You know, you only need half of the detergent that they tell you you need." If you do as much laundry as we do, this tip will save you money right away. If you miss the smell of lots of detergent, add an extra half of a dryer sheet to the dryer. You can also use half the amount of dish detergent in your dishwasher!

THE BEST PLACES TO FIND CLOTHES ONLINE

Shopping online is one the easiest, best ways to save money on clothing. Here are some of our favorite sites to find good, inexpensive clothes on the web.

• 15dollarstore.com is exactly what it sounds like—a store where all clothing is $15 or less. In addition to a large selection of women's clothing, the site also has belts, handbags, sunglasses, watches, jewelry, and some children's clothing.

• If you're trying to save money, obviously it's probably a good idea to try to stay away from designer fashion labels. But if you just can't help yourself, Bluefly.com is the best place to go for a bargain. You'll find discounted prices on men's and women's designer clothing, including such labels as Kenneth Cole, Burberry, Armani, Marc Jacobs, Calvin Klein, and Prada. Just try to keep it to a couple outfits and a handbag!

• One of our favorite sites for children's clothes is Childsclothingoutlet.com, which has high quality children's clothes for reasonable prices. They also carry books and gifts for kids and parents as well.

• At Zappos.com, you'll find more shoes than you ever imagined possible, including men's, women's, and kids' sneakers, dress shoes, boots, and sandals. The best part is that they also send you a return shipping label, so if you don't like the shoes you've ordered, you can easily return them for free.

• If you love looking at new styles in magazines, check out Gojane.com. They have a special section called "As seen in…" that highlights recent fashions in popular magazines and offers them for discounted prices.

CUT YOUR CLOTHING CLUTTER

Are you afraid you'll be buried in a fabric avalanche every time you open your closet? It's time to take control of your wardrobe. Going through your clothes and figuring out what you have and what you don't need has a lot of money-saving benefits. First of all, you can take unwanted clothes to a resale shop and either make some money or exchange them for new clothes. Secondly, you'll have a better handle on what clothes you need for the season, cutting down on duplicates and making impulse buying less likely. If you tend to buy a lot of items that are similar to each other, try organizing your closet by color, so when you pause by that black polo shirt at the store you'll remember just how many black short-sleeved shirts you own.

SAVE WITH STEAM

Save time and money by steaming your clothes at home rather than taking them to a dry cleaner. Choose a steamer with 1,200 to 1,500 watts of de-wrinkling power—anything above that may cause a short circuit, and anything under that may not be effective. Hang suits, shirts, and skirts on a shower rod and steam several items at once. You may find it doesn't take too much longer than dropping them off at the dry cleaner's!

WHO KNEW?

Only about 10 percent of shoppers prefer to buy clothing on the web. When surveyed, many people cited not being able to try clothes on as the main reason why they'd rather shop in a store. It was also found that the younger you are, the more likely you are to buy an outfit online.

YOUR OWN PERSONAL SHOPPER

At Shopittome.com, you enter your favorite brands and they do all the online searching for you. When items come up for sale on a department store's site, they'll send you an email, alerting you to the discount. The best part is, you can specify your size, so you won't have to waste your time wading through links only to find that the store is all out of extra-large!

...AND NEVER TO RETURN!

Did you know that up to 30 percent of consumers never get around to returning items that they meant to take back to the store? If you're unsure about an item while you're in the dressing room, the best thing to do is to simply not buy it. Once we began following this policy, we were shocked at how few never-worn garments ended up in our closets.

TAKE IT TO THE TAILOR

Going to a tailor may seem like an expensive proposition, but it's often worth it if you unearth a good deal on a suit or other clothing that doesn't quite fit. Found some jeans for ten bucks that look great but are an inch too long? A jacket that's a steal, but a bit too baggy in the arms? For a small price, you can get these items custom-fitted at a tailor. And you'll still be saving a ton from what the normal retail price would be.

LET'S START AT THE VERY BEGINNING

How many times have you purchased an $80 sweater, only to find a nearly identical one for much less later? When you begin to look for clothes for the new season, always start at the least expensive store first. Since most clothing stores carry similar items each season, you'll make sure to get each piece for the best price. You should also try to buy most of your basics—solid-color t-shirts, socks, and so forth—at the cheaper stores. Save the expensive stores for the uniquely designed and patterned clothes, where you can see the difference in quality.

KEEP YOUR CLOTHES LASTING LONGER

Once you've found the outfit of your dreams, make sure it lasts! Here are some tips to prolong the life your favorite clothes:
• Many of your clothes can be worn several times before you wash them, especially sweaters. Most items get more wear and tear from being in the washing machine than they do on your bodies!
• Turn knitted clothes and t-shirts with designs on them inside-out when washing and drying.
• Synthetic fabrics wear faster, naturals like linen and wool will last longer.

• When pre-treating a stain, try to wash the item within an hour after applying the stain remover.

• When ironing clothes, especially dark ones, iron them from the inside. Make sure to use distilled water if you use a steaming iron to prevent stains.

• Line dry your clothes. Not only is air-drying less harsh, you'll love the real smell of sun-dried linens. If you don't have a clothes line, hang shirts and pants on hangers on tree limbs! Just make sure not to put brights in the sun, as they may fade.

GET THRIFTY

Many people are intimidated by shopping at thrift shops. What's the best way to wade through all those clothes, organized in no particular order? How do you know you're getting something good? And what should you be wary of? First of all, it's more intuitive than you might think. If you're browsing through a thrift shop and the clothes seem dingy or dirty, find a different shop. But for the most part, you'll find perfectly good clothes that are simply one or two seasons old. Make sure to check each item closely for rips or stains, and keep in mind that it may be worth it to buy something if you think you can easily repair it. Many resale shops are organized by the color of the clothing, but most also use some kind of color-coded tag system (so that all items with a red tag are 50 percent off, for instance). Best of all, you can usually exchange your clothes for money or store credit. Make sure to ask if the store offers you more "money" for your item if you opt for credit rather than cash. And have fun looking for bargains! You never know what fantastic find you're going to get at a thrift shop.

WHO KNEW?

Edna Woolman Chase, the former editor in chief of *Vogue* magazine, once said, "Fashion can be bought. Style, one must possess."

EVERYONE HAS A PARTNER

When your kids' socks finally need to be thrown away because of holes, rips, or stains, make sure to keep their mates. Since you probably bought them in a pack, it's only a matter of time before another one just like it bites the dust. And if you end up with mismatching socks, your kids can still wear them around the house or to bed.

KNOW THE CODE

Ever go to buy something online and see that little box to enter a promotional or coupon code? Well now you never have to wish you had something to enter into that box again. At Retailmenot.com, you can find hundreds of codes that will give you savings at a large variety of websites, including Kohls.com, Amazon.com, and JC Penney online. If this site doesn't have a code for the store you're looking for, also try Momsview.com, Dealtaker.com, or Pocketdeal.com.

TURN EXTRA-LARGE INTO EXTRA-STYLISH

If you're like us, you have a million XL t-shirts that you've gotten from various organizations and events. Unfortunately, all of them make you look like a formless blob. Fix them into something you would actually wear by getting a little creative. Simply cut a scoop neck to make a great shirt to wear over a bathing suit, or make a fitted tank top by cutting off the sleeves, slicing up the sides, and restitching to fit your form. For instructions on how to perform these t-shirt surgeries and many more (most of which don't even require a sewing machine), check out the book *Generation T* by Megan Nicolay. And make sure to get it for free at the library!

BEFRIEND THOSE IN THE KNOW

If you have a favorite shop you find yourself spending a lot of time in, make sure to get friendly with the sales staff! Clothing stores often have unannounced sales, but if you're down with the people that work there, they'll often you tip you off. And if they really like you, they may let you put an item on layaway until it goes on sale a few days later.

chapter **6**

BEAUTY ON A BUDGET

STRONG FOUNDATIONS

Some of the most expensive kinds of make-up are foundation and powder. Make it last longer by buying a shade darker than your natural shade, and then mixing it with moisturizer (for foundation), or baby powder (for powder) until it matches your normal color. You'll have more than twice as much, and you'll never be able to tell the difference!

FACE MASKS FOR EVERY SKIN TYPE

Face masks aren't only good for your face, they're a relaxing treat. Make girls' night even more interesting by making your own! With these homemade face mask recipes, you'll get the same results as store-bought, and they're easy, too!

• Simple avocado: Just mash up a ripe avocado (the fruit shouldn't be tough, and it give a little when touched). Apply to your face and let set for 15 to 20 minutes. Add some cucumbers to your eyes for extra relaxation! Rinse with warm water.

• Go bananas: Bananas are great for oily skin. Mash one banana with a teaspoon of honey and a couple of drops of lemon juice. Apply to your face and let sit for 15 minutes before washing with a cool washcloth.

• The solution for dry skin: Mix one egg yolk with a teaspoon of honey and teaspoon of olive oil. Leave on your face for as long as possible, then wash off. The vitamin A in the egg yolk is great for your skin!

• Tastes pretty good, too: Mix ¼ cup brown sugar with 1½ tbsp of whole or 2% milk. Rub into your face, then leave on for 10 minutes. The brown sugar will exfoliate while the milk will moisturize.

• You won't believe it till you try it: Clay cat litter is actually the exact same clay that's found in some of the most expensive face masks on the market. Find some cat litter labeled "100% all-natural clay" and mix it with water until it gets to the consistency you want. Adding a couple drops of scented oil will also help make it seem less like you're applying cat litter to your face. Wash the mask off after it hardens.

• Skin soother: This face mask is perfect for sunburned or irritated skin. Combine ¼ cup full-fat yogurt with 2 tbsp of oatmeal. Mix vigorously for one minute, then apply to your face. Leave on for at least ten minutes, then wash off with warm water.

TRIM ON THE CHEAP

If you're used to getting an expensive haircut, it's hard to switch to a bargain salon such as Supercuts. But what you can do to save yourself hundreds of dollars a year is to get a hairstyle that doesn't need a lot of upkeep. When you need a trim in between cuts, go to an inexpensive salon. While hair stylists at the bargain salons sometimes can't give you the fancy cut you want, they can usually handle a simple trim, following the path of your normal stylist. If you just need your bangs cut, ask at your usual salon if they offer free bang trims in between cuts.

YOUR SITE FOR SALON SAVINGS

Addicted to fancy shampoo? Find all the same brands you buy at your salon for much less at Salonsavings.com. Shampoos and hair-care products are 10 to 80 percent off, and skincare and fragrances are offered at much less as well. This site is also a great place to check if you have a favorite beauty product that has been discontinued.

WHO KNEW?

According to a report called "Beauty at Any Cost" by the YWCA, American women spend a total of $7 billion dollars a year on cosmetics—an average of $100 per person per month. If invested for five years, that monthly $100 could pay for a full-year's college tuition!

SHAVING SECRET

Instead of buying expensive shaving creams or foams, try shaving with hair conditioner. (Buy the cheapest kind.) The conditioner will soften the hair and provide a layer of protection between your blade and your skin. You'll even find your shave is closer.

WHO KNEW?

It is estimated that up to 50 percent of the cost of a perfume is simply to pay for its advertising and packaging.

AND YOU MIGHT WIN A CAR!

If you really want to save money on cosmetics, consider becoming an Avon or Mary Kay representative. You may find you have enough friends and co-workers who are interested in their make-up, skincare, and other products to make it easy and worth your while. Meanwhile, you'll get their high-quality cosmetics at wholesale prices.

KNOW WHAT TO LOOK FOR

When trying to compare a cosmetic with a less-expensive one, you only have to look at one thing: the active ingredients list. Products that have the same active ingredients are going to do almost the exact same thing, even if the percentages are a bit off. (The only thing you might have to worry about is which smells better.) You'll be surprised how many expensive brands—especially of hair products like shampoo—have the exact same chemicals in them for vastly higher prices.

NEVER PAY TOO MUCH FOR MAKE-UP

When shopping for make-up and other cosmetics, never ever shop at department stores! Because of commissions for the salespeople and the cost to rent the space at the store, they're never a bargain. Instead, check out your local grocery store or discount store such as Wal-Mart or Target—they almost always have the exact same brands for much less. If you can't find them

there, try to find a cosmetics discount outlet such as Sephora or Ulta, or search for "discount cosmetics" online. If you still can't find your brand, consider switching to another brand you *can* find. Choose one a good friend uses, and ask her if she'd be willing to buy it from you if you don't like it. It shouldn't be too hard to find one you like just as much that costs much less.

THE TRUTH ABOUT MOISTURIZERS

If you're looking for a way to cut back on cosmetics, the first place to start is with your moisturizer. Whether it's night cream, day cream, anti-aging lotion, or anti-wrinkle solution, it's all pretty much the same. Pick a moisturizer with an SPF of at least 15—other than that, go with a less expensive brand whose smell you like. Your wallet will know the difference, but your face never will.

AT THE END OF THE DAY...

For an inexpensive way to remove mascara, eye liner, and shadow, try baby shampoo. It contains many of the same ingredients as eye-make-up remover, and works just as well. Dispense a small amount on a tissue or cotton ball, rub over closed eyes, and rinse with water.

WHO KNEW?

You might be reassured that a "hypoallergenic" product won't cause problems for your sensitive skin, but the term actually doesn't mean much. Companies put this word on cosmetics that they think are less harsh than others, but there are no federal regulations guiding the use of the word. Most dermatologists agree than a product labeled as "hypoallergenic" is no different from a product without the label—if you can even find one.

GOOD MAKE-UP DOESN'T HAVE TO BE EXPENSIVE

For a great deal on cosmetics on the web, head over to Eyeslipsface.com, where they have everything from lip gloss to nail polish for only a dollar apiece. They also have a great "gifts" section, with cute box sets for unbelievable prices. For instance, eye shadow, mascara, eye liner, a brush, and an eye lash curler for only $5!

YOUR HAIR WON'T KNOW THE DIFFERENCE!

For a cheap alternative to hair gel, try a light hand lotion instead. Especially if you have a short cut, it works great to weigh down curls and frizzies, and costs less than half the price. Hand lotion is also great as a hair product because you can find it in so many scents—you'll probably find one you like even more than your normal hair-care product!

STYLISTS IN PROGRESS

Get your haircut on the cheap by students who are studying to be beauticians. You may risk a less-than-professional 'do, but it's probably better than having a friend do it. Student haircuts are also great for kids, whose simple cuts are usually hard to screw up. To find a beauty school near you that offers cuts and styles at low prices, go to Beautyschooldirectory.com.

TAX-SAVING TIPS

7

On average, people who file their tax returns early receive $200 more in their refund. Unfortunately, this is a cause more than an effect—people who file early tend to do so because they know they're getting money back and want it sooner!

TURBO YOUR TAXES

If your taxes are getting complicated enough to get confusing, but you don't want to go to an accountant, try purchasing a software called TurboTax (available for download at Turbotax.com). Turbo Tax walks you through your taxes by asking you questions, and does all the math for you. It'll let you know if you're eligible for credits and even help you itemize your deductions. It's definitely worth the $30 to buy!

TAKE CREDIT WHERE CREDIT IS DUE

Believe it or not, there are lots of parts of the tax code that basically give you back money. If you pay someone to take care of your child, pay tuition to a school, or have made your home more green, you are probably eligible for at least one tax credit. Make sure to read the instructions with your tax return carefully, typing the name of a line and schedule into google or another search engine if you can't figure out what it's saying. (Or to save yourself a huge headache, just go speak to an accountant or use a software program like TurboTax.) Taking all your credits will bring your taxes down and your refund up!

HELP IS ON THE WAY!

When tax time comes around, don't despair: there are plenty of places to turn for help. Here are some of the useful sites for hints and advice on your taxes.

• Smartmoney.com is a great site for any kind of financial information, but we especially love their tax section. Find it by holding your mouse over "personal finance," and then click on "taxes."

• At Taxprophet.com, find straightforward information about in-depth tax issues and questions like "Do you really owe taxes on your babysitter?" Click on "General Tax Information" and then "Tax Class" on the left-hand side to see a list of topics, then click on one of the topics to see articles rated as "basic," "intermediate," and "advanced." The site also has a great section for foreign taxpayers.

• Did you know that the IRS actually publishes a guide of tax hints for each year? It's geared towards tax professionals, but much of it is pretty easy to understand. To find the guide (which is in pdf format), go to Irs.gov and type "publication 4437" into the search box.

• If you're having problems with the IRS—any problems—you have to check out Taxhelponline.com/solver.htm, which offers information about twenty-nine distinct problems, from not having the receipts that show your deductions to "The IRS claims I earned income I did not report."

SAVE ON TAXES WHILE YOU SAVE FOR COLLEGE

Our favorite section of the Internal Revenue Code is number 529. (What? You don't have a favorite section of the IRC?) Section 529 is all about saving for college, in accounts called "529 plans." With these savings accounts, you can put money away to use for college or college-related expenses such as textbooks and room and board. These plans aren't subjected to federal (and some cases, state) taxes, and some states even offer matching contributions into the fund. For more information about 529 plans, including the different types of plans, fees you may incur, and where you can sign up for one, visit Sec.gov/investor/pubs/intro529.htm.

WHO KNEW?

April 15 isn't just tax day. It is also the anniversary of the first air mail flight, which took place in 1918 between New York and Washington, DC (with a stop-over in Philadelphia). The air mail service, part of an army program to train pilots, was only supposed to last a year. The planes left once a day, every day but Sunday, and each carried approximately 300 pounds of first-class mail.

BECOME YOUR OWN BUSINESS!

These days, it's easy to start a business. And why not? If you can make money selling something, you can file as a "sole proprietorship" to claim that income...and don't forget the deductions! For example, if you enjoy quilting, start a business selling quilts online. (Two good sites for selling homemade goods are Etsy.com and Cafepress.com.) You can now deduct many of the expenses relating to making the quilts you're trying to sell. For more information, go to Finweb.com/taxes and click on "Sole Proprietorships" and "Business or Hobby?" on the left-hand side.

NEED AN ACCOUNTANT?

If the schedules, forms, booklets, and rigid tax language is making you want to scream, don't despair. There are many free tax counseling services that will help you sort out your W-2s from your 1040As. Ask at your local library or community college about local tax help, and find out if your state offers free tax assistance programs. You can also call the AARP tax helpline at 1-888-687-2277 or visit them online at AARP.org/taxaid. And remember, if you end up having to pay anyone to help you with your taxes, you can deduct this cost on your form!

GIVE A LITTLE

Did you know that you can give a tax-free gift of up to $12,000 each year ($24,000 for you and a spouse)? This is a great way to reduce your estate tax or pay into a loved one's 529 college savings plan. For more information, visit Irs.gov and type in "publication 950" into the search box.

WHO KNEW?

Seventy-seven percent of Americans say they "hate" financial planning. OK, I guess we did know that one.

FILING FOR YOUR FILING

The most essential step for saving money at tax time is an easy one: make sure to stay organized. Keeping receipts (especially the ones you have to print out) and keeping them filed will ensure that you don't lose track of the expenses and deductions you've accumulated throughout the year. Without all that sorting to do, you'll also be more likely to not put off doing your taxes to the last minute—and the earlier you file, the more quickly you get your refund back!

DEDUCT THIS!

The easiest way to pay less taxes is to make sure to take all of the deductions possible. If you itemize your deductions, here are some expenses that will help your bottom line.

• Moving expenses. If you start a new job after you move (50 miles or more), you can deduct your movers, moving van rental, airfare and lodging when interviewing for jobs, and even the cost of a storage facility.

WHO KNEW?

The Libertarian Party, the third-largest political party in the United States, campaigns on a platform of repealing all income taxes and abolishing the Internal Revenue Service.

• State and local income taxes. You can deduct the entire amount you had to pay on your State return.

• Sales tax. If your state doesn't require you to pay income tax, you can deduct the amount you've spent on sales tax in the past year. It's a lot of adding and receipt-saving, but think of the money you'll save!

• Jury duty payments. If your company continued to pay you a salary while you were on jury duty, and you had to sign over your wages to them, you can deduct these wages.

• Health and dental expenses. You can deduct anything you paid out-of-pocket for health or dental care, as long as these expenses exceed 7.5% of your gross adjusted income. This number is easier to get to than you might think, even if you haven't had a major surgery. You can include health, vision, and dental insurance premiums, travel expenses to the doctor or hospital, prescriptions, over-the-counter dental supplies, all hospital expenses including meals, eye glasses, and much more.

• Teaching supplies. If you're an educator, you can deduct up to $250 in supplies, even if you don't itemize.

• Charitable contributions. Even small stuff adds up. Don't forget anything you did for your church or child's school, like bake cookies (you can deduct the ingredients!), or travel expenses when you are volunteering.

SAVINGS FOR YOUR HOUSE AND CAR

chapter

8

LOOK FOR LEAKS!

According to the Environmental Protection Agency, a well-sealed home can be up to 20 percent more energy efficient. Most leaks occur in the basement or attic—look for where you feel a draft or around wiring holes, plumbing vents, ducts, and basement rim joints. You'll be able to seal lots of leaks with a simple caulking gun, but for instructions on how to plug larger holes go to Energystar. gov and search for "plug leaks."

MAKE THE MOST OF THAT EXPENSIVE GAS!

With gas prices as high as they are, it's worth it to try to use the least amount of gas possible when driving. Here are some tips to get the most out of your mileage.

• Keep your tires inflated. It's much harder for your engine to get your car to move when your tires are even a little flat. Invest in a gauge, and make sure to keep them as inflated as possible without over-inflating.

• Go manual. If you're buying a new car and can't afford a hybrid, consider going with a stick-shift rather than automatic. Manually changing gears saves energy because your car is only using as much energy as it needs to—it's never in a higher gear when it shouldn't be. Being able to coast down hills also saves you tons.

• Stay under the speed limit. Your car will begin to lose fuel efficiency once it gets over 60 m.p.h. One of the easiest ways to save money on gas is to always go the speed limit—and it's safer, too.

• Change your oil regularly. As oil ages, it gets thicker and harder to push through the engine, causing more energy to be used. By changing your oil regularly you'll make sure you get the best fuel economy possible.

• Remove excess weight. Take anything heavy out of your trunk or back seat that doesn't need to be there (kids don't count). An extra 100 pounds in your car can decrease your miles per gallon by 2 percent.

• Pick the best route. Stopping and starting and going up hills will cause you to use more gas. Consider taking a route that will allow you to make less adjustments as you are driving, even if it takes a little longer.

• Roll up your windows on the highway. Having the wind streaming through your hair might be fun, but it increases drag on the car and makes it take more energy to run. In this case, it's actually usually cheaper to run the AC.

• Group your errands. Obviously if you're driving less distance by not traveling from home each time you'll save on gas, but the Department of Energy also reports that several short trips beginning from a cold start use almost twice as much energy as a single trip of the same length. Keep your engine warm and your car won't have to work as hard.

PUT 'EM TO WORK!

Want to know how to never have to pay for a car wash again? Make the kids do it! All you need is a bucket, a few squirts of car-washing detergent, and some sponges. Then put the kids in their swim-suits and get out the hose. Kids will love the water and suds, your car will get clean, and they'll be tired by bedtime!

NEGOTIATE YOUR WAY TO SAVINGS

If you're lucky enough to live in an area that has more than one company providing phone, cable, or other utilities, use this to your advantage by lowering your payment amount—without having to switch companies! Find out what the competitors are charging by calling them or visiting Whitefence.com, then call and ask for your rates to be lowered. If the first person you talk to says no, don't be discouraged and don't be afraid to ask to speak to a supervisor. If you call between 9 a.m. and 5 p.m. you'll be more likely to get an experienced supervisor on the phone who's willing to bargain.

WHO KNEW?

When asked to rank the status of their household finances, 53 percent of respondents rated them as "bad," "very bad," or "terrible." And unfortunately, only 5 percent of people said they thought the situation was getting any better.

INSURANCE POLICY

Save while you protect

BUY IT A JACKET

A water-heater insulation jacket costs from $15 to $35, but it can cut your costs to heat your water dramatically. By insulating your water heater, you'll cut down on the amount of energy it needs to use to heat standing water in half, also cutting down on the amount you need to pay.

SAVE MONEY FAST ON HOMEOWNERS' INSURANCE

Did you know that most homeowners' insurance policies will deduct 3 to 5 percent for adding simple security features such as a smoke alarm or dead bolts? You can often save a lot more if you're willing to install a more sophisticated security system. These systems can get expensive, but the savings may be worth it. Before you choose one, make sure to call your insurance company to see what kind of system they recommend. You may also to be able to save if you are 65 or over.

TWO THUMBS UP

For fun wall decorations for kids' rooms or a family room, frame movie posters from your family's favorite movies. Try asking at video stores or movie theaters if you can have their posters when they are done with them. Often, they'll just give them to you for free. If you're looking for an older movie, you can also find them inexpensively on the internet. Just type in the name of the movie and the word "poster" into google or another search engine. Another inexpensive decoration option is buying old magazines and hanging vintage ads and photo spreads in frames.

SAVE ON CALLS OVER THE WEB

Using your phone over the internet may sound daunting, but it can save you hundreds of dollars a year. In addition, it can provide you with some nice benefits, like choosing your area code and getting voice-mail messages sent to your email inbox. Some voice-over-internet phone services have to be used through your computer, and other companies will provide you with an adapter that you use to connect your phone and your computer (or router). CNET.com has one of the best guides to internet calling. To find it, type "cnet internet phones" into google and click on the first link.

FINDING THE BEST DEALS ON FURNITURE ONLINE

The internet is a great place to turn for reasonably priced furniture. When buying online, the furniture normally comes in boxes, so you usually have to spend a lot of time assembling, but for big savings it's worth the wait. Here are some of our favorite furniture sites.

• If you've been living on the planet Earth for the last few years, you've probably heard of IKEA. But what you may not know is that IKEA.com has much of the same merchandise as the store, for the same great prices.

• The best thing about Greatpricedfurniture.com is that they have *free* shipping. They also have special categories for budget furniture and sale items. This is great place to look if you're looking for furniture for an entire room.

• Babydirect.com is an excellent source for baby products, and they also have great deals on baby

HOW TO LIGHT UP A ROOM

If you have the interior decorating bug, but don't have much to spend on home accents, here's an easy way to add ambience to a room: use Christmas lights. Great over a doorway, winding up a large houseplant, or along a counter, you'll be surprised how many compliments you'll get for this simple technique. Especially great to implement in January, when all the holiday decorations are half off!

and children's furniture. Click on the links on the left-hand side for "Baby Furniture," "Nursery Room," and "Kids Furniture." And make sure to check out their princess and fire truck beds for toddlers!

• If you're looking for used furniture locally, the best place to check is Craiglist.org. Select your city and then find "furniture" under "for sale." You'll find great prices on all sorts of furniture for sale by its owner, but you normally have to figure out how to transport it yourself.

CO-OPS AREN'T JUST FOR GRANOLA-EATERS ANYMORE

A fuel co-op is an organization that negotiates lower rates for your gas by buying in bulk. Even though you normally have to pay a membership fee, you can save big bucks on your heating bill by joining a fuel co-op, and you often don't even need to change from your normal gas company. Most co-ops will offer you discounts if you're a senior citizen or are on a fixed income. To find one in your area simply type in "fuel co-op" and your geographic location (e.g. "New Jersey") in google or another search engine.

RAISE YOUR DEDUCTIBLES TO LOWER YOUR COSTS

You can save hundreds each year on your home and auto insurance by raising your deductibles. If you have more than one type of insurance with the same carrier, you may also qualify for bundled discounts. It's not in your insurance company's best interests to keep you informed about the lowest rates, so make sure you call them and ask.

NOT PERFECT, BUT MUCH CHEAPER

Let's be honest. If you have kids, your furniture is going to be banged up. So why not get deep savings on furniture that already has a few dings on it? All furniture stores sell floor samples of their merchandise. Ask a sales representative if the store is willing to sell the floor samples; often, stores have sales specifically for floor samples and the salesperson can tell you when that happens. Otherwise, they may only be willing to sell the floor sample if it's the last piece left. Ask if you can leave your phone number for when the rest run out, and don't be afraid to bargain on the price!

COLD IS BETTER

Did you know that 80 to 90 percent of the energy used by a washing machine is to heat the water? When doing laundry, always use cold water to wash your clothes. Due to advances in detergents and washing machines, the only time you really need to use warm or hot water is when you need to get a really bad stain, like red wine or oil, out of an article. Not only will you help the environment, you're save money on heating the water, too!

WHEN IT'S TIME TO CLEAN UP YOUR ACT...

Making household cleaners from common ingredients is not only much less expensive than buying them at the store, they are also more natural, and usually better for your home. Here are a few easy cleaners that will surprise you with their ability to make things shine as well as the store-bought kind.

Of course, there are thousand more tips like this in *Who Knew II!*

A PAIN IN THE DRAIN

Make sure to drain your water heater once a year to get rid of sediment. Left too long, this grit can build up until you're using energy to heat sludge. To find out how to complete this simple home maintenance trick, type "how to drain a water heater" into google or another search engine. And start to save!

YOUR GUIDE TO GAS

Before you go to the gas station, visit Gasbuddy. com. Enter your zip code, and your new buddy will tell you the gas stations with the cheapest prices nearby. You can also search to find the least expensive pump prices in your entire state or entire city. You'll never fill up, only to see a cheaper station on the way home, again!

TOO BAD THERE'S NO GETRIDOFMYBILLS.COM

At Lowermybills.com, you'll find a way to reduce just about any bill. Whether you're looking to refinance your home, consolidate your credit card debt, or just lower your phone bill, this site will give you the tools you need to compare different companies and calculate your costs. You can also sign up for an email newsletter filled with tips and deals.

WHO KNEW?

All told, Americans drive over 245 billion miles per month.

• For a great all-purpose cleaner, mix ½ cup of borax with 1 gallon of water.
• A teaspoon of olive oil mixed with ½ cup white vinegar makes a great furniture polish.
• Use baking soda on a sponge to get grime off of tubs. Add cream of tartar to get rid of the green spots water can leave behind on cobber tubs.
• To clean your floors, mix a gallon of warm water with white vinegar—½ cup for linoleum and ¼ cup for wood.

WON'T YOU BE MY NEIGHBOR?

Do you and your neighbors both use wireless internet?
A great way to save is to share an internet plan. If you already have a plan, ask a neighbor you trust if they'd like to pay you for half the cost if you give them the password to your network. Especially if you live in an apartment building, you should be able to use the wireless internet hub you currently own, but if your homes are particularly far apart you may need to extend your network with a second hub or router.

THE VENETIAN SECRET

Be smart when using your heating or air conditioning. When the heat's on, open the blinds on windows that are exposed to the sun, and use a little solar heat to help out your furnace! When you have the AC going, close as many blinds as possible, so that the sun won't get in and warm your house more than necessary.

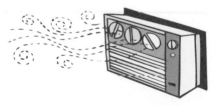

FREE

SALE

GET YOUR COUPONS HERE

Here are some more sites you should make sure to check out: Coupons.com, Fatwallet.com, Couponcabin.com, Wow-coupons.com, Shortcuts.com, Coolsavings.com, and 8coupons.com (which is a terrific site for those of you in the New York City area.)

WHO KNEW?

In 2007, 89 percent of Americans said they used coupons, up 3 percent from the previous year.

THE BEST PLACES TO FIND FREE STUFF!

It's easy to get product samples for free over the internet. Here are some of our favorite sites for getting free stuff—visit them often and make sure to use an email address you don't mind getting lots of junk mail at. Don't enter personal information like your social security number, and make sure the site is reputable if you are entering credit card info. Otherwise, enjoy all the deals the internet has to offer!

• Freesampleforger.com gathers together give-aways from around the web and provides direct links for you to click to claim them.

• If you're a dog lover, check out Workingdogweb.com/freestuff.htm for lists of free canine-themed items and supplies for your pet.

• At Freeafterrebate.info, you'll find deals from sites offering merchandise that comes with rebates. Mail in the form or fill out the information online and get your money back!

• Visit Freesamplesblog.com for information about free product samples, coupons, and give-aways happening at stores nationwide.

• At Dailyedeals.com/free_stuff, freebies are sorted by free product samples; free merchandise such as t-shirts, gift cards, and cosmetics; free after rebate; and offers to make easy money. Some of these links are more reputable than others, but it's definitely worth a look.

• Totallyfreestuff.com has so many links to freebies it's hard not to be overwhelmed! They gather everything here, so if you look for freebies on a daily basis this is a good site to find offers you didn't find elsewhere.

• If you have a baby on the way, go to Fitpregnancy.com/freebies to find sweepstakes and freebies from the popular magazine and across the web.

• Yofreestuff.com specializes in links to free gift cards, household products, food samples, and pie-in-the sky freebies like big screen TVs, which often require you to make purchases online or sign up friends for junk mail.

THE POWER OF FOCUS

When they need to know what real people think about their products, companies hire focus groups to try them and then share their opinions. Being in a focus group can get you free product samples, a bit of cash, and the opportunity for your voice to be heard! Sign up to be part of a focus group at Greatopinions.com, where you enter information about yourself and then are contacted by a representative when there is focus group work available in your area. Or go to Findfocusgroups.com, which culls focus group opportunities from around the web that you can apply for directly. Either way, you should know that many focus groups won't hire you if work in the marketing industry, have any connection to the company the product is made by, or say that you have participated in a focus group in the last six months.

MEDS FOR LESS

If you don't have a prescription plan, or if your prescription plan has denied you coverage for an expensive medication, you may be able to get it for free or at a deep discount. Check out Needymeds.com for ways to get the medicine you need from the government, private outreach programs, and even the pharmaceutical companies themselves. Just simply find the name of your medication and see if you qualify! You should never be without the prescriptions you need.

LIVE TO LEARN

At GCFlearnfree.org, you can finally learn how to use all those computer programs that have been befuddling you. Sign up for classes taught over the internet, or download learning materials to go at your own pace. Classes include Microsoft Windows, Word, and Excel, internet searching, and email basics. The site also offers free lessons in managing money, math skills, and "everyday life" problems.

NEVER BE AFRAID TO COMPLAIN

If you're unhappy about a product, you should always write to the company to tell them so. The address can usually be found on the wrapper, and if there's only a web address their mailing address can be found on their website. Mail a letter explaining why you're unhappy with the product and include the wrapper or label, if possible. Most companies will send you free samples of similar products or replace the product you purchased if it was faulty.

KEEP THE KIDS ENTERTAINED

At Freestuff4kids.net, self-avowed "cheapskate mom" Randa Clay gathers all sorts of things for kids online. Some links are to cool, interactive sites that your child will enjoy, some are to online giveaways of kid-related products, and others will give you free printable worksheets and games for kids. To never have to buy a coloring book again, head over to Free-coloring-pages.com, where you can find printable images for kids to color, including those of popular cartoon characters.

PARTY HARDY

Tupperware parties have been going on since the '70s. But there are now lots of different kinds of parties you can host in your home: Pampered Chef kitchen products, Partylite candles, and Petal beauty products, to name a few. These companies offer you freebies and discounts to host parties in your home, and some will even offer you money based on how much your friends buy. Try to be informed about the products ahead of time so you can recommend them to those who attend. But remember, parties should be fun! Make sure not to pressure your invitees too much, and provide snacks and drinks for everyone while they're perusing the goods.

THE SEED SOLUTION

The best source for free seeds for you garden is... your garden! When your flowers start to dry up each year, make sure you check them for seeds that you can replant. Marigolds are an especially good treasure trove for abundant seeds—let the flower tops try out, peel them open, and you'll find hundreds of future marigolds ready to plant. When next spring rolls around, if you don't have enough seeds from last year, buy them from the nursery rather than buying small plants in dirt. The seeds are much cheaper, and you'll have more fun watching them grow from scratch.

GIMME, GIMME!

Here's a secret not many people know: companies want to give you their products for free. More specifically, their new products that they're hoping you'll tell all your friends about. Keep your eyes open for new types of candy, cosmetics, soda, and snack foods. Visit the company's website or look on the product's label to find the company's address. Write a letter (which usually works much better than an email) saying how interested you are in the product and ask if you can have a free sample. For faster processing, write the name of the product on the outside of the envelope. This doesn't always work, of course, but you'll be surprised how much free stuff you'll get in the mail!

SHUTTLE TRANSPORT

Once you start looking for them on the road, you see them everywhere. No, not bad drivers—free shuttle buses. These buses run from hotels to airports, malls to Main Street, and even sometimes to large, big-box stores like IKEA. They usually keep a regular schedule (driving in a loop) and are often mostly empty. If you're going somewhere close to a shuttle bus, why not score a ride for free? Most shuttle bus providers don't mind you hopping aboard even if you're not going to or coming from their exact destination, but it's not a bad idea to check, especially at hotels. (Some hotels will let your ride for a price.) You may find it's one of the cheapest ways to get to the airport—or to your friend's house, next to the mall.

WHO KNEW?

The business practice of giving stuff away is often called "freeconomics." Freeconomics has been on the rise due to the low costs of doing business on the internet, and the belief that if someone gets something from for free, they will come back for more. Will you?

WHO KNEW?

King Gillette, the inventor of the disposable razor, was unsuccessful at selling his invention until he started giving the razors away for free. Soon, everyone wanted to buy the disposable blades.

MYSTERY SHOPPING: BECAUSE YOU'VE ALWAYS BEEN THE MYSTERIOUS TYPE

Mystery shopping can get you free products and a bit of money on the side, but most of all it's downright fun. Visit a store, then fill out an online survey about your experience. The pay isn't much—usually not more than $15—but you'll be reimbursed for products as varied as designer sunglasses to lunch and a beer at a restaurant. If you're interested in mystery shopping, be careful of online scams. You should never have to pay to be a mystery shopper! The best site to trust is that of the Mystery Shoppers Providers Association. Visit Mysteryshop.org/shoppers to find mystery shopping and focus group opportunities near you, and find out more about this fun side job!

TURN YOUR HOBBY INTO FREE STUFF

Interested in books? How about reviewing them? Like scrapbooking? How about teaching people tips and tricks to make their scrapbooks look as good as yours? Taking your hobby online is a

KICK THE HABIT FOR FREE

Trying to quit smoking? You're on the way to savings already. But did you know that you can often obtain smoking cessation products such as nicotine gum and patches for free? Many states and cities offer free products or reimbursements, especially if you are on a fixed income. Also check with your employer, school, or health insurance company to see if they offer free products. And think about how much you'll save when you don't have to buy cigarettes anymore!

great way to start getting free stuff. (Hey, you can even make a site about your love of getting things for free!) Visit Blogger.com to easily set up a name and address for your blog, and pick colors, type, and an overall look. If you can get a lot of readers to your blog, you can write to companies asking for samples of products for you to review on your site. They get free publicity, and you get free stuff!

SWEEPSTAKES SECRETS

Who doesn't love a good contest? Instead of buying a lottery ticket each week, put yourself in the running to win big by spending a little time each day or week entering online sweepstakes. Here are some tips to help you get that new car/ exotic vacation/lifetime supply of beef jerky of your dreams.

• Make an email address just for contests. When entering many contests, you are also signing up for a lifetime of junk mail. Just make sure to sift through the junk carefully in case you're notified of a win! It's usually pretty easy to tell the difference.

• The biggest, best source for contests around the web is Online-sweepstakes.com, which has sweepstakes organized by type, new, and expiring soon.

• If you're only interested in the really big bucks and prizes, visit Helpingmomsconnect.com/contests.htm. The great thing about the links on this site is you normally don't have to do anything to win—just sign up.

FIND FREEBIES NEAR YOU

Find loads of items on sale near you that are FREE after a mail-in rebate. Just visit Salescircular.com. Enter your zip code and you'll be directed to a list of products by type—electronics, apparel, appliances, etc.—that are on sale in your area. Click on "Free After Rebate" and get a list of items that you can get for free, from make-up to software.

FROM YOUR MAILBOX TO YOUR INBOX

One of our favorite magazines for money-saving tips is *All You*, and now you can get a free sneak peek at the savings they have in store for each issue. Visit their website at Allyou.com and sign up for their email newsletter by clicking on "Sign up for the ALL YOU newsletter now!" on the bottom right side. In addition to offering tips and tricks, the email will tell you all of the coupons that are going to be in that month's issue, so you can plan ahead.

• For smaller contests that often require you to submit something or comment on a site, try Contestguide.com and Contestformoms.com. If you have a special talent like writing or art, type in "writing contests" or "art contests," for instance, into a search engine to find even more opportunities.

• Check for exclusions. Many contests will exclude people from a certain state. These left-out states are your gain (assuming you don't live in one!), because if less people can enter, your chances of winning will go up. Also look for contests with particularly high age requirements or that are just for one gender.

• Bookmark sites of contests you can enter again. Use your internet browser or a bookmark-site like Delicious.com to keep track of contests that allow you to enter more than once. Many allow a click a day, and some give something away each week and restart. If you have a lot of sites to keep track of, try organizing them in folders based on how much you want the prize or how often you can enter.

• Avoid any contests you think a lot of people will enter. Remember, the name of the game is trying to up your chances of winning by lowering the number of contestants. If a sweepstake has been advertised heavily or has a really long entry period, avoid it. Likewise, if you find a contest held by a local business or that has a short entry period, your chances will go up.

• Only enter contests you trust. When entering a contest, you should never have to enter credit card information or your social security number. It's best to only enter contests from companies or sites you recognize.

ALL POINTS TO FREE ATMS!

Sick of paying up to two dollars every time you have to visit an ATM? At Allpointnetwork.com, you can find all of the surcharge-free ATMS in your area by entering your city and state or your zip code. Many of the listings are for stores that offer cash-back with purchase, but you never know when you'll find a free ATM you never knew about.

DISCOUNTS ON THE GO

At Cellfire.com, you can sign up to get coupons sent directly to your cell phone! Browsing the dozens of offers is easy with a built-in organizer application. Many deals you call to receive, but others you simply get on your screen and then show to the cashier at stores as various as Hollywood Video, Caribou Coffee, Subway, and Gamestop. This is a perfect activity for when you're waiting around to pick up your kids!

WHO KNEW?

No one actually knows who was the first person to say "The best things in life are free."

LUCKY BE A LADY...

For a great deal on designer jeans or just to have a little fun, check out Luckybuckoff.com. Play a quick game online, and you can win 20, 25, or 30 percent off a pair of Lucky Brand jeans at Luckybrand.com or in one of their many stores nationwide.

NOTES

chapter 10

OTHER WAYS
TO MAKE MONEY
AND SAVE

WHO KNEW?

Most banks are FDIC insured, but you should still make sure yours is. With an FDIC-insured bank, even if the financial institution fails your money will still be insured for up to $200,000.

SAVE AUTOMATICALLY

To help you save on a monthly basis, make it easier to contribute to your savings account. Banks allow you to set up recurring transfers, so set one up for each time you get paid. Putting even $50 into your savings account each time you get a paycheck will quickly add up, and you'll be glad you have it on a rainy day or when vacation time rolls around.

HAGGLING 101

Sure, you've always been able to haggle at car dealerships and mom-and-pop stores. But did you know that "big box" stores such as Home Depot and Best Buy are getting in on the act, too? With sales slipping, the staffs of chain stores are now being told that bargaining is OK. Here are some tips to make sure you get the most bang for your buck.

• To add extra ammo to your asking price, do a little research at competing stores or on the internet beforehand. If you can tell a salesperson that a store nearby is offering the same item for less, you'll be more likely to get it at that price.

• Be aware of "extras" that competing stores are offering. Even if you're not interested in an extended warranty or free engraving at the other place, you can use the incentive to your advantage when bargaining.

• Take a spouse or friend. One of the best methods for negotiating is the "good cop, bad cop" strategy. One of you acts really interested in the product, while the other continually points out the flaws and negative aspects. Because of the "good cop," the salesperson will remain hopeful that he can sell the product, but "bad cop" will make him work for it.

• Find stores where there is no commission. If the salesperson stands to make less on a product, then he will be less likely to give it to you for less. But if it's only company money that's being lost, there's a higher chance he'll bow to your demands.

• Buy accessories, too. Most stores have a higher mark-up on accessories for well-selling items. If you're buying a memory card and a carrying case for your new camera, you're more likely to get a discount on the camera itself.

LEGALESE

If you need legal advice on any issue, make sure you take advantage of free legal assistance offered to you. Call or visit the courthouse and ask about free legal services, which are often offered by local law schools or non-profit organizations. Many law firms will also offer you a free consultation. Of course, the point of the consultation is to try to get you to use their services, but you don't have to! Go prepared with a list of questions and write down the answers. Do as much research as you can on the internet by googling the type of case and the name of your state. If your case goes to court, don't be afraid to ask clerks or the judge if you don't understand something.

CHECK IT OUT

When pawing through the coupon inserts in your Sunday paper, make sure to save the advertisement for checks. Buying checks through private companies aren't just for people who like cartoon characters next to "pay to the order of." They're also for people who like to save! You'll always get them more cheaply than simply ordering them through your bank, and don't you give your bank enough money as it is?

A PARTY IS ABOUT THE PEOPLE...

...Not how much money you spent on it. Before you throw a huge bash, write out your priorities in terms of what you think is most important to spend your money on (for example, the least on decorations and the most on booze). Then figure out how much you're willing to spend on the highest item on your list, and work your way down. Friends always ask, "Can I bring anything?" and you shouldn't be afraid of asking your good friends to bring a dessert or appetizer. And don't forget—pot lucks and picnics are cheap and always popular.

PAY LESS FOR SHIPPING

If you're wondering what the fastest, cheapest way to ship an item is, head over to Shiptool.com. You enter the weight of the package, your address, and were it's going to, and Shiptool will give you quotes from Fed Ex, UPS, the United States Postal Service, and DHL. The site also provides free tracking and direct links to the carriers once you've seen the prices.

WHO KNEW?

Dorothy Parker once said, "If you want to know what God thinks of money, just look at the people he gave it to." Remember: money isn't everything!

WAIVE IT OFF

It sounds too simple to be true, but you can often just ask credit card companies, utilities, landlords, and others to waive late fees. If you're a longtime customer with a good history, companies will often re-credit your account, especially if it was your first offense.

SWAP THEM OUT

When you notice your kids getting bored with a toy (and they always do), don't buy them a new one. Instead, stash the disfavored toys away in a bag or box. Once you have several toys, swap with a friend for toys her kids have gotten sick of. Not only will you save on money, you'll save on the clutter of continually purchasing new playthings for your kids.

YOU'VE DONE PLENTY FOR THEM…WHAT CAN THEY DO FOR YOU?

Your employer may offer more perks than just weak coffee in styrofoam cups and free filtered water. In addition to the traditional retirement accounts and healthcare options, many employers—especially companies that have a national presence—offer many more benefits on a small and large scale. Check with your HR department to see if you can get pre-tax money for transportation or "flex-spending"—funds that you can spend on medical or other specified expenses. Many employers often have agreements with businesses and are able to offer their employees discounted movie and amusement park tickets, savings on cell phones and computer equipment, and cheaper rates at nearby gyms.

EBAY: WHAT IS IT AND HOW DOES IT WORK?

Simply put, Ebay.com is a fast and fairly easy way for you to make money and find inexpensive products. You can post photos and information about a product you want to sell, and other users can buy it. Anything goes: jello molds, clothes and accessories, musical instruments, baby products, computers, DVDs, cars, even a piece of toast that looks Jennifer Lopez. (To see a list of their offerings, click on "categories" on the upper-left.) When you're doing the purchasing, you can either bid on items, or select the "buy it now" feature. Bidding takes a little longer, but can save you a lot of money. For more information, click on "help" on the upper-right-hand corner, where you can find an easy-to-understand guide to getting started and frequently asked questions.

GOOGLE: IS THERE ANYTHING IT CAN'T DO?

Google isn't just for the internet anymore. Now if you need information on-the-go you can text google with your cell phone. This is especially useful for addresses and phone numbers. Simply type in the business name and your city or zip code and text to 466-45 (G-O-O-G-L). This service is also great for settling bets: type in "Mt. Everest elevation" and get the answer instantly. Or text "weather" and your zip code to get a three-day forecast. You can also call 1-800-GOOG-411 for free directory assistance. Normal rates for your plan apply, but you won't be charged any extra.

STOP PAYING FOR UNUSED MINUTES

If you find yourself under-using your mobile minutes each month, consider canceling your current plan when your contract runs out and paying as you go instead. With pay-as-you-go, you pay an amount of money up front instead of getting a bill each month. Most plans will charge you from 5 to 10¢ a minute, and offer discounts if you put a large amount of money—usually $100—on the phone. The good news is that you can also use text and picture messages, and sometimes even web surfing, on the phone. The bad news is that the minutes usually expire after a certain amount of time. Pay-as-you-go phones are great for phones that you pretty much only use in an emergency, and for giving to teens so that you can make sure they don't overspend. Ask at a cell phone or electronics store about pay-as-you-go phones and promotions.

BUY AT AUCTION

Every month hundreds of cars and other merchandise are confiscated by the police. And hey, just because a criminal used it, it doesn't make that $100 laptop any less useful. Look in the classifieds section of your newspaper to find local auctions, or check out Propertyroom.com to find unbelievable deals on tools, electronics, bicycles, video games, and more, not to mention some truly bizarre items like a Freon tank, "assorted copper tubing," night vision goggles, and an adorable cement frog. If you're in the market for a car, try Policeauctions.com or Seizecars. com. And if you're OK with not telling the recipient where it came from, auctions are also one of the least expensive places to buy beautiful jewelry and gemstones.

The internet is an amazing source for money-saving tips. Simply google "ways to save money" and see all the great ideas that turn up.

AN OCTOBERFEST FOR YOUR HOME

If you're looking to buy large appliances or household furnishings like a washing machine, dryer, dishwasher, refrigerator, or sofa, the best time to buy is in October. At this time of year, businesses are busy making room for their holiday inventory, so you'll find tons of sales on last year's merchandise. Go ahead, celebrate a little early!

WHEN HEALTH INSURANCE GOES WRONG

Those of us lucky enough to have health insurance love having to pay less for healthcare—as long as the system works. If (OK, *when*) you have problems with your health insurance reimbursing you for a claim, it can be so frustrating and even demoralizing that you're tempted to give up. Here are some steps you can take to make sure you get the money you deserve.

• Stay organized. Take notes when you are disputing a claim, and refer to them when you call the company. The representative will be more likely to take you seriously if you can state the dates you spoke to someone, what the claim or reference number is, and the amount it was for. Also make sure to have the date the service was performed and the date the claim was submitted on-hand.

• Ask your doctor for help. If the insurance company is telling you the procedure wasn't necessary or "reasonable or customary," have your doctor's office write a letter or call the company to explain why it was.

• If you have a group plan, see if you can get the administrator of the plan (usually in your HR department) to help you complain to the company.

• Contact your state's department of insurance. If they won't help you go after the company, they can usually at least provide you with important information about your rights.

• Don't be afraid to go to court. If you feel you are unjustly being denied a claim, a court will probably think so, too. If the claim amount is less than $500, you will most likely not need an attorney, but if it is higher than that, many attorneys will take the case on a contingency basis (meaning they only get paid if you do) if it seems strong. Bring any literature from the company that seems to contradict why they have been telling you the cost wasn't covered—in most states, judges have ruled that policies have to be straightforward enough for a layperson to read them, not an insurance agent or lawyer.

LEARN TO LOVE HOME-COOKING

If you're used to eating out a lot, it's hard to break the habit. But because of all the money eating out eats up (please excuse the pun), it's worth it to try to cut back. Make it easier on yourself by doing your shopping on a different day than you actually prepare the food—that way you aren't stacking up the chores of buying groceries and making dinner. Plan ahead and try to make enough food to take to work with you for lunch the next day, saving even more. Encourage yourself to cook by inviting over a friend, then having dinner at her house the next week. Once you see all the money you save, not calling the pizza parlor three nights a week will be easier.

YOU'RE SUSPENDED!

Many newspapers and magazines will allow you to suspend your home delivery or subscription. If you're going on a long vacation, make sure to call them up and stop service for while you're away. You can also often do this for online movie rental and other services. You won't miss them while you're gone, and then you'll get an extra week or two when your subscription would normally be up.

A HANDY TIP

Especially if you've got kids who never seem to know when enough is enough, add water to your hand soap. Your hands will get just as clean, but the soap will last longer! You can also find foaming soap dispensers at a lot of stores, which are also good for keeping the amount of soap you use to the minimum you need.

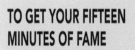

TO GET YOUR FIFTEEN MINUTES OF FAME

Ever wanted to see if you could win some money on TV? Go to Starnow.com or Talenthunter. com to search for opportunities in your area to be a movie or TV extra, try out for a reality show, or be a guest on a talk show. And don't forget us when you become famous!

SHARE YOUR HINTS AND TIPS WITH US!

Do you have a great hint or tip to help save money or time? Share it with us! If we feature it in our next revision of Who Knew? or our next book, we'll be sure to include your name next to the hint.

Just email us at **hintsandtips@castlepointpub. com**, and please include your contact information so we can reach you if we decide to include your submission.

To reach us by mail, just send your hint to:
Hints and Tips
Castle Point Publishing
PO Box 1090
Hoboken, NJ 07030

Don't forget to include your return address or email address.

And thanks for your help!

INDEX

B

Books, 17, 18, 36, 66
  free books, 17
  inter library loan, 17
  libraries, 17
  magazines, 17, 29, 37, 56, 68, 77

C

Car maintenance 54, 55
  car interest, 57
  changing oil, 54
  cheapest prices, 59
  dealership, 57
  driving, 54, 55
  fuel efficiency, 48
  gas station, 59
  inflated tires, 54
  save gas, 54, 55, 57, 58, 59
  speed limits, 54
  stick-shift, 54
  usage of gas, 54
  washing, 55
  windows, 55

Clothes
  best deals, 36
  buying, 36, 37
  children, 36
  clothing clutter, 37
  designer fashion labels, 36
  email alerts, 38
  fashion trends, 37
  ironing, 39
  knitted, 38
  laundry, 36, 59
  line dry, 39
  prolong life, 38
  sales, 40
  shopping online, 36
  socks, 38, 39
  stains, 39
  steamer, 37
  synthetic fabrics, 38
  tailor, 38
  XL t-shirts, 40

Cosmetics
  baby shampoo, 45
  beauty products, 64
  buying, 42, 44
  deals, 43, 44, 45
  hair gel alternatives, 46
  hypoallergenic, 45
  make up remover, 45
  make-up last longer, 42
  moisturizer, 42, 45
  prices, 43, 44, 45, 46

Credit card
  agreement, 11, 13
  air mile programs, 12
  bad debt, 11, 14
  balance transfer, 13
  buying appliances, 76
  clean credit, 14
  collection agencies, 13
  collections, 13
  consumer debt, 11
  credit debt, 10
  credit limit, 12, 13
  credit reallocation, 13
  credit report, 10, 11, 13, 14
  date of payment, 12
  debt consolidation, 12
  discounted loans, 12
  free balance transfers, 12
  free counseling, 11
  lawsuits, 13
  manage budget, 11
  offers, 12, 13
  payments, 12, 13, 14
  reducing debt, 11, 12, 13, 14, 60
  secondary card holder, 10
  shopping, 36
  student loans, 12

F

Free and consolidated things
  bookmarking sites, 10, 16, 23, 25, 36, 48, 50, 57, 62, 68
  canine theme items, 62
  consumer grievances, 10, 11
  contests, 67, 68
  coupons sent to cell phone, 69

  deals on designer wear, 69
  disposable razor, 66
  focus groups, 63
  free shuttle buses, 65
  free stuff, 62, 65, 66, 67
  freebies, 62, 63, 64, 67
  freeconomics, 65
  garden seeds, 64, 65
  give-away, 17
  learning computer programs, 63
  magazines, 17, 20, 37, 56, 68, 77
  mystery shopping, 66
  online coupons, 62
  prescription plan, 63
  Product samples 62, 63
  products, 27, 30, 31, 32, 43, 44, 57, 63, 64, 65, 66, 67, 74
  rebates, 62
  sales, 18, 36, 40, 52, 59, 72, 76
  smoking cessation products, 66
  surcharge-free ATMs, 69
Tupperware parties, 64

Furniture
  buying online, 57
  free shipping, 57
  used furniture, 57
  great deals, 57
  floor samples, 59

G

Grocery
  buying meat, 32, 33
  buying, 30, 31, 33
  canned vegetables, 30, 34
  coupons, 30, 31
  deals, 30
  discount wholesaler, 30
  disposable products, 31
  dog food, 34
  free items, 30, 31, 33
  free seasoning, 33
  generic products, 30
  growing a spice garden, 33
  self service grocery, 34
  substitute soda, 32
  thrift shops, 31, 39

Grooming
    face masks, 42
    hair stylists, 43
    haircuts, 46
    shaving, 44

H

House maintenance
    air conditioning, 60
    appliances, 56, 67, 76
    buying gas, 29, 31, 54, 59
    deductibles, 58
Environment Protection Agency, 54
    home and auto insurance, 58
    household cleaners, 56
    household finance, 55
    inexpensive decoration, 56
    insurance policies, 56
    internet phone services, 56
    internet plan, 60
    lighting, 58
    payment amount, 55
    reduce bills, 33, 58, 60, 75
    security systems, 56
    washing machine, 36, 38, 56,
    59, 76
    water-heater, 56

M

Money saving tips 68, 76
    accessories, 72, 74
    appliances, 56, 67, 76
    auction, 75
    bargaining, 72
    bidding, 74
    commission, 72
    contingency basis, 76
    coupon inserts, 73
    court, 14, 73
    disputing claims, 49
    eating out, 77
    extras, 12, 72
    FDIC-insured bank, 72
    free directory assistance, 75
    health insurance, 66, 76
    HR department, 74, 76
    legal advice, 73
    mobile minutes, 75
    money saving tips, 68, 76
    negotiate, 3, 52, 55

    parties, 64
    pre-tax money, 74
    recurring transfers, 72
    research, 72, 73
    shipping, 37, 57, 73
    soap usage, 77
    suspending home delivery or
    subscription, 74
    swapping toys, 74
    waive late fees, 74
    winning money, 68

Movies and Music
Movies 18, 20
    DVDs, 17, 18, 19, 74
    free screenings, 17
    free, 16, 17
    movie lending circle, 18
    movie theatre's revenue, 20
    rentals, 18
    spending, 20, 31

Music 16, 17
    deals, 16, 17
    free downloads, 16
    free Mp3s, 16
    free tracks, 16
    itunes, 16, 19
    online radio station, 17
    pod-casts, 19, 20
    radio shows, 16, 19

S

Shopping
    baby products, 57, 74
    buy online 62, 63, 64
    deals, 30, 36, 57, 60, 62
    returning items, 38
    shoes, 36, 37
    thrift shops, 31, 39

T

Tax
    advice, 48
    business, 49
    charitable contributions, 52
    code, 42, 44,
    counseling services, 45
    estate tax, 50
    filing, 51

    financial information, 48
    financial planning, 52
    health and dental expenses, 52
    Internal Revenue Code, 49
    jury duty payments, 52
    moving expenses, 52
    negotiate, 52
    pay less, 52
    sales tax, 52
    software Turbo Tax, 48
    state and income tax, 52
    tax day, 49
    teaching supplies, 52

TV
    cable systems, 18
    shows, 16, 18, 19, 20, 22,
    watching, 19

V

Vacations and Activities
    camping, 25
    car and hotel rental discounts,
    22, 25
    deciding factor, 22
    discount packages, 26
    discounted areas, 27
    food and souvenirs, 27
    free museum admission , 22
    see sports, 25
    show tickets, 22, 23
    TV taping, 22
    vacation packages, 24
    volunteering for free admission,
    22, 25

Local and national theme parks,
Disney World, 26
    group discounts, 26
    merchandise tie-ins, 26
    package deals, 26
Travel Industry Association, 26

Travel
    best deals online, 27
    cheapest days, 23
    deals on student's ID card, 24
    rental car deals, 25, 51
    train fare discounts, 22
    transportation and lodging, 22